HAYNES EXPLAINS
FOOTBALL

Owners' Workshop Manual

© Haynes Publishing • Written by **Boris Starling**

Published in October 2017

A catalogue record for this book is available from the British Library

ISBN 978 1 78521 156 0

Haynes Publishing, Sparkford, Yeovil,
Somerset BA22 7JJ, UK
Tel: +44 (0) 1963 440635
Website: www.haynes.com

Haynes North America, Inc.,
861 Lawrence Drive, Newbury Park,
California 91320, USA

Printed and bound in Malaysia

Cover image from Getty Images

Illustrations taken from the
Haynes Rover 213 & 216
Owners Workshop Manual

Written by **Boris Starling**
Edited by **Louise McIntyre**
Designed by **Richard Parsons**

Safety first!

Like all sports, football has its hazards. Injuries can be caused by receiving an ill-timed tackle, making an ill-timed tackle, falling over the ball, falling over a dog who's wandered onto the pitch, running into the goalposts, being accidentally elbowed in the face by a teammate, being deliberately elbowed in the face by an opponent, failing to warm up, failing to warm down, and so on. All in all, much safer to watch it from the stands or on TV.

Working facilities

Take a deep breath…. The pitch must be rectangular with the goal lines 45–90m long and the touchlines 90–120m long; the inner edges of the goalposts must be 7.32m apart and the lower edge of the crossbar 2.44m above the ground; the six-yard box is, er, six yards up the pitch and six yards from each post, the penalty area 18 yards in the same configuration and the penalty spot 11m from the goal… you may now breathe.

Contents

Introduction

Football is the most popular sport in the world. It's simple, for a start, with far fewer rules than many other sports (by comparison, it takes an average of 83 minutes to explain rugby to a novice, 271 minutes to explain American football, and three weeks to explain cricket). It's easy to play – all you need is a ball, an area and the traditional jumpers for goalposts. It has a defined time period, though this is subject to Einstein's theory of relativity: 90 minutes can feel like 90 seconds when watching Barcelona or Brazil, and like 90 hours when watching England. The ball's in play for a lot longer than it is in other sports. Most of the skills on display are visible to even the most casual observer.

As with many sports, football as we know it was invented by the English. Normally with sports we invent, such as rugby and cricket, we like to keep the number of countries who play it down to a minimum (mainly the ones we used to rule) so we have a fighting chance of winning now and then. No such chance with football. Hence the 51 years* of hurt.

About this manual

The aim of this manual is to help you get the best value from football. It can do this in several ways. It can help you (a) decide what work must be done (b) tackle this work yourself, though you may choose to have much of it performed by external contractors such as the young bloke at work who looks like he might be quite lively in the office five-a-side team, the grizzled old coach who still dresses in his original 1970s adidas tracksuit, the old dear who's been making the tea for the past six decades and without whom the place would fall apart, and the keen nerdy guy who's always on refereeing courses and will probably be running the line at Wembley in a few years' time.

The manual has drawings and descriptions to show the function and layout of the various components. Tasks are described in a logical order so that even a novice can do the work. Don't run before you can walk. Don't dribble before you can run. Don't nutmeg before you can dribble. And don't showboat, ever, unless you want to be clattered hard by the opposition's most psychotic player and told 'we don't do that round here, sunshine.'

* Number subject to limitless increase.

⚠ Dimensions, weights and capacities

Overall height

5'6"	Of the tricky little pocket battleship with a low centre of gravity.
6'2"	Of the midfield general with physical presence and a great engine.
6'7"	Of the gangly beanpole target man (Peter Crouch).

Overall weight

80kg	Of a footballer in peak condition.
90kg	Of a footballer suffering enforced injury layoff and with a penchant for chocolate bars.
100kg	Of a recently retired footballer who thinks he can still eat like he was in full-time training.

Consumption

2017	porridge and fruit for breakfast; salmon and quinoa for lunch; chicken and vegetables for dinner; water and electrolytes to drink.
1977	full English breakfast: burger with extra fries for lunch; chicken tikka masala and pilau rice for dinner; 10 pints to drink.

Engine

Stroke	the way a cultured footballer passes the ball. Or what a manager's liable to suffer if he doesn't calm down.
Power	plenty behind a well-struck shot, which the goalkeeper's glad he's got nowhere near as it would have taken his head off if he had.
Torque	of transfers, twice a year. 99% of it is ill-informed and plain wrong. Not that anyone remembers or cares.
Bore	the bloke in the corner of the pub who tells you repeatedly that it's not like it used to be, there's too much money in the game, if these lads weren't earning millions they'd be stacking shelves.
Redline	when you've been fouled for the 14th time in a row and the ref still hasn't brought out a yellow card and now you're going to take the law into your own hands.

Model range

A football team has 11 players. Aside from the goalkeeper, whose position and role are fixed, the 10 outfield players can be arranged into a variety of formations. For ease of reference, we have defined them in the classic 4-4-2 line-up.

1. Goalkeeper
You don't have to be mad to work here, but it helps. Men apart, in every way – allowed to use their hands while in their own area, equipped with gloves and encouraged to sport strips so lurid they can be seen from space and/or double as hi-vis gear. Usually the last to be picked for the team.

2. Right back
Keen on putting in the 'reducer' (heavy and deliberately late tackle on the fancy-dan winger he's marking). Always gets 6/10 in the match report, even if he's scored a hat-trick. Can be either reluctant to venture forward (which annoys the midfielder in front of him) or all too keen to do so (which annoys his fellow defenders.)

3. Left back
Like the right back, except left-footed. All left backs have two patron saints: St Stuart of Pearce and St Julian of Dicks, erstwhile hard men of Notts Forest and West Ham respectively.

NO-NONSENSE HARD MEN **FLASH HARRYS AND FANCY DANS**

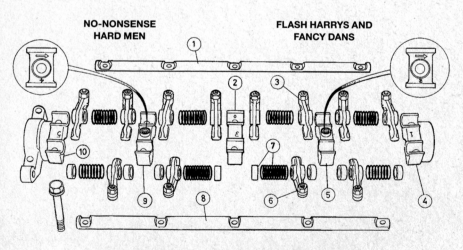

FIG 12•1 **FROM 1-11: HOW THEY ALL FIT TOGETHER**

4. Centre midfield

Often deemed the 'defensive midfielder', which means he hangs back to protect the defence while number 8 goes upfield and gets all the glory. Not that 4 minds. No, he doesn't mind a bit. And he'll show how much he doesn't mind by leaving unspeakable things in 8's kitbag.

5. Centre back

Tall, good in the air, and world-class at pointing and shouting. Likes: robust challenges before clearing the ball into the fabled Row Z. Doesn't like: cheeky little strikers who run rings round them, target men who lead with their elbows when jumping for headers.

6. Centre back

Just like '5'. Enjoys going forward for corners and making a nuisance of himself in the opposition penalty box. Centre backs work in pairs: Nemanja Vidic and Rio Ferdinand, Fabio Cannavaro and Alessandro Nesta, Hale and Pace, Cannon and Ball.

7. Right midfield

Convinced he can bend it like Beckham, even if the only thing he's bending is the ringpull on a can of lager. Keen on taking the ball to the byline, losing control of it, and appealing for the corner anyway despite the fact that the nearest defender was in the next county.

8. Centre midfield

Thinks he's the best player in the team, irrespective of whether or not this opinion is justified. Covers every blade of grass, be it real or artificial. If he's a good player, this means he offers valuable help in both attack and defence. If he's not, this means he gets in as many people's way as possible.

9. Striker

He sees himself as the poacher, the fox in the box, the finisher. His teammates see him as a selfish glory hunter who toe pokes the ball in from three feet and then acts like he's just recreated Maradona's famous goal against England in 1986.

10. Striker

Aware he's wearing football's most sacred number, and therefore that he has to be twice as good as everyone else just to ensure they don't laugh at him. Who he'll blame if things aren't going his way: his fellow striker, his midfield, the fickle hand of fate.

11. Left midfield

Just as his counterpart on the right can't bend it like Beckham, so too this cove can't gallop like Giggs. Well, he can, but only if you were watching Giggs on slow motion and this bloke at normal speed. Likes to try stepovers. Usually does one too many and falls over.

Vehicle capabilities

Whenever you see a manager gesticulating wildly on the touchline, it's because his team have taken all those precise tactical instructions he's spent weeks preparing and forgotten every single one of them the moment the game has begun. (Mike Tyson put it another way: 'everyone has a plan till they get punched in the mouth.') Knowing that manufacturers of whiteboards and marker pens would go bust without managers up and down the land using their products, here's a guide to some of the more common tactics seen on a football pitch.

SEEKING THE POSITION OF MAXIMUM OPPORTUNITY

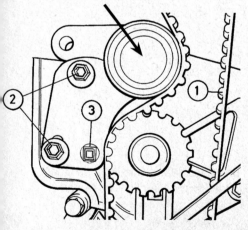

FIG 12•2 **BIG COGS, LITTLE COGS: THE TACTICAL MASTERMIND**

Total Football
In which usual formations are abandoned in favour of players constantly rotating positions and filling in wherever they are needed. This of course depends on having players good enough and versatile enough to play this way. If the players aren't up to it, Total Football quickly becomes Total Shite.

Pass and move
In which the team keeps both players and ball in motion as often as possible, offering more options in attack. Claimed as 'the Liverpool groove' by the Liverpool side before the 1996 FA Cup Final (which they promptly lost). Often seen in the first ten minutes of a park match. Rarely seen in the last ten minutes of a park match, by which time the players are in a state of semi-comatose exhaustion.

Through ball
In which a midfielder plays the ball between the defenders for a striker to run onto. Looks wonderful when it comes off. When it doesn't, a rigid routine of mutual blame must be followed: the striker must accuse the passer of overhitting the pass while the passer accuses the striker of being too slow to react.

Long ball
If you're Dutch, a pinpoint 60-yard pass which finds its intended target with military precision. If you're English, a hopeful punt upfield which you claim as genius on the odd occasion it actually finds someone wearing the same shirt colour as you.

Triangle
Playing the ball between three players to move the ball forward without losing possession. Not to be confused with (a) the most pointless musical instrument out there (b) a so-bad-it's good early 80s soap set on a North Sea ferry (c) a loosely defined oceanic region where aircraft and ships are said to have disappeared.

4–2–3–1 formation
In which full backs provide plenty of support to the wingers in front of them while a lone striker leads the line. Not to be confused with Ted Rogers and Dusty Bin of '3-2-1' fame.

Zone defence
Midfielders and defenders form lines across the field to deny the attackers space. Good: 'in the zone', switched on and concentrating. Bad (unless you're 4-0 up with 10 minutes to go): 'chillout zone'. Worst: 'erogenous zone'. On a football pitch? In the middle of a match? Wearing polyester? You need help.

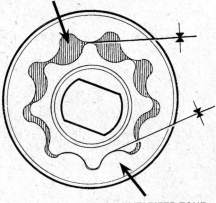

THE TWILIGHT ZONE

THE DEMILITARIZED ZONE

FIG 12•3 **UNPICKING THE ZONAL DEFENCE SYSTEM**

Man-to-man marking
A defender picks his man and follows him wherever he goes. Done properly, this will eventually prove extremely annoying for the man being marked, especially if the defender taps him on one shoulder and then appears at his other shoulder, repeats whatever he says, or sings a selection of Backstreet Boys hits over the course of the match. Man-to-man marking was a favourite of hardmen Italian defenders in the 1970s and 1980s: none more so than the fearsome Claudio Gentile who kicked Diego Maradona from pillar to post in the 1982 World Cup and, unrepentant, said afterwards: 'signor, is no dancing school.'

Warning lights

Football matches are controlled by a referee, who has to put up with constant questioning both from the players ('ref, did you see what he did to me there?') and the spectators (who enquire loudly and repeatedly as to (a) the identity of the onanist in the dark colours (b) the last time said onanist acquainted himself of the services of an optician).

The referee is helped by two assistant referees, who anyone over the age of 40 will still insist on calling 'linesmen'. The linesmen (I am 47) can advise the referee in instances where the referee hasn't seen an incident (perhaps because he should indeed have gone to a high street optician as advised by 22,829 spectators), but the final decision rests with the referee.

At higher levels of football there is also a television match official who, like a security guard on a night shift, spends most of his time watching old de Niro movies on an ancient set and now and then has to pretend he was paying attention.

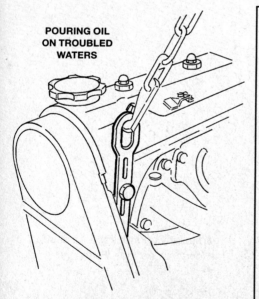

POURING OIL
ON TROUBLED
WATERS

FIG 12•4 **KEEPING FIRM CONTROL:
A REFEREE'S METHODOLOGY**

'Why do you do it?'

The question most referees are asked sooner or later is 'why do you do it?' Who would voluntarily choose to stand in the middle of several thousand people giving them fearful abuse? Surprisingly, the answer 'because I am a masochistic martinet' is rarely given. Referees at all levels talk of the pleasure they take in building a rapport with players, of the buzz they get from making correct decisions and of the increased confidence and strength of character it gives them in other areas of their lives.

⚠ Referee sanctions

Referees have several options available in the case of foul play:

a) Awarding a free kick against the offending team. For direct free kicks near the area, referees now have natty little cans of foam which they spray on the ground to mark the line beyond which the defenders cannot advance till the kick is taken. It's only a matter of time before (a) a ref mistakes this can for his shaving foam (b) decide to add other items to their waistband in the same way police officers carry truncheons etc.

....

b) Awarding a penalty when the offence takes place in the penalty area. A minimum of two minutes is needed between blowing the whistle and the penalty actually being taken for the defending team to protest, act outraged and mime scenes from the most overwrought of Italian operas.

....

c) Showing a yellow card for a foul which is more serious than just a free kick but not in itself enough to show a red card and get the player sent off, though I'm watching you from now on sunshine, you can bet on that.

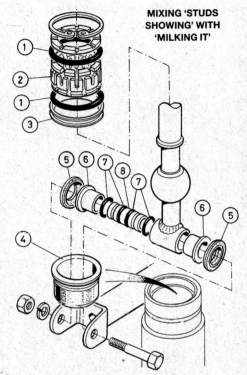

MIXING 'STUDS SHOWING' WITH 'MILKING IT'

FIG 12•5 **THE RED/YELLOW CARD ALGORITHM**

d) Showing a red card either for a particularly bad foul or for a second yellow-card offence. Some red cards are so obvious that the player doesn't even wait to see it, instead walking off of their own volition while applauding the crowd.

Weekend driving

The Premiership may get 95% of the attention, but the league matches up and down the country every Sunday are far more reflective of real-life football. Sunday leagues come with their own set of shouts, characters and details. Typical Sunday league details:

a) No team ever has exactly matching kit. The shirts will all match, but someone will always wear their own pair of shorts or socks. Kit will either smell mouldy – because whoever was supposed to wash it didn't – or else like a Persil factory as it's been washed by a man who has no idea how to use the washing machine.

b) People still smoke. Especially the players. Especially at half time.

c) Everyone turns up an hour late the morning after the clocks go forward and an hour early the morning after they go back.

d) Changing rooms and the public car park are often one and the same.

Celebrations synchronised to within an inch of their lives and copied off something someone had seen on YouTube

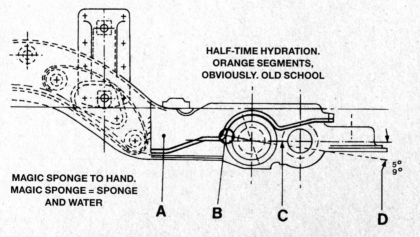

HALF-TIME HYDRATION. ORANGE SEGMENTS, OBVIOUSLY. OLD SCHOOL

MAGIC SPONGE TO HAND. MAGIC SPONGE = SPONGE AND WATER

A   B   C   D

5° 9°

FIG 12•6 **SUNDAY BLOODY SUNDAY – GETTING THROUGH 90 MINUTES UNSCATHED**

⚠ The Sunday League XI

Character	Description
The Show-Off	Has bright yellow and pink boots, fancies himself as a trickster, and might as well be wearing a 'KICK ME' sign around his neck – because inevitably that's exactly what half the opposition will do.
The Really Good Ringer	Doesn't look that prepossessing when you see him slink onto the pitch. Looks pretty good once he's stuck his fifth goal in and it's not even half-time yet.
The Psycho	Will be either obviously so (large, shaven head, tattoos) or less obviously so (small, wiry, modelled on Begbie from *Trainspotting*). The latter is of course even more dangerous than the former.
The Bloke Who Had A Trial	What he's failing to add is that it was at Snaresbrook Crown Court rather than Crystal Palace.
The Club Treasurer	No one ever pays their subs too. Ends every season hundreds of quid out of pocket.
The Tall Bloke	Alternates between centre-back and striker.
The Ginger Bloke	Quietly desperate for the others to nickname him 'Scholesy'. It's never going to happen, mate.
The Taxi Driver	Spends the two hours before the match not in quiet contemplation of the task ahead of him but driving round the neighbourhood picking up those who've overslept and/or found themselves the night before in beds that aren't their own (whether those beds belong to young ladies or the local police station).
The Seeper	The one who drank so much last night that you can smell the alcohol as it seeps from his pores.
The Fat Man	May once have been quite good. Hard to tell now. Puts an unholy amount of strain on his shirt front.
The Shouter	Always bellowing instructions at his teammates and yelling at them for their mistakes. Bellows all the louder when he makes a mistake himself.

e) Warm-ups involve people chatting while knocking the ball around between themselves. A couple of rash souls perform pre-match stretching exercises. These guys are always the first to do their hamstrings once the match starts.

f) The tricky winger isn't slaloming to avoid would-be tacklers. He's dancing his way through a minefield of dog turds.

g) Spectators must always comprise in equal ratios (a) the abusive (b) the very abusive (c) uninterested family members.

h) Someone trying to do a bicycle kick. And missing. By miles.

i) Car interiors looking like the Somme after all the muddy boots have been there.

j) The overpumped ball which on a cold morning really really REALLY hurts when someone kicks it hard into your thigh.

k) The sliced clearance from a centre back which flies into his own net and which no keeper on earth could have stopped.

l) 3G can mean both a type of mobile data network and a type of astroturf pitch. The first is very useful for finding out why half your team haven't turned up at the second.

FIG 12•7 **MAINTAINING OLD AND WORN JOINTS – AN ESSENTIAL MEDICAL GUIDE**

⚠ Sunday League shouts

Shout	Description
'Have a dig!'	To any player within 30 yards of goal, notwithstanding that the odds against him scoring from that range are roughly the same as those concerning an Elvis comeback.
'How long, ref?'	First asked within 10 minutes of the start, and then every 5 minutes with the increasing desperation of men whose fitness is in inverse proportion to their waistlines.
'Name on it!'	When a ball drops towards two or more people who could reasonably be expected to head it. Pedants like to point out that the 'name on it' is usually Adidas, Nike, Umbro or similar.
'Stay on your feet!'	To any defender who has failed to learn the lessons of the previous 38,376 times he's slid into a tackle and missed by yards.
'We're not talking!'	Bemoaning the lack of communication between team members. Usually because said team members are having trouble breathing, let alone talking.
'We're still in this!'	No, you're not. You're 6-0 down and there are two minutes left. (Though this could be said with an air of sardonic resignation, in which case it will raise a smile.)
'Got two here!'	When you're having to mark two players as someone on your team can't be bothered to track back. Rather passive-aggressive and therefore to be encouraged.
'Watch the runners!'	Exhortation to your defenders to beware opposition players coming from deep. Often obeyed in the most literal sense – they do indeed watch the runners without making much effort to stop them.
'Man on!'	There's a bloke behind you about to tackle you. No, he's not about to tackle you. He just has tackled you.
'Away!'	The ball is near our goal and no one has the skill to play it out of danger among themselves. Therefore let's hoof it upfield and try to regroup before they attack again.

Model variations

Barcelona's motto is 'more than a club'. In truth, every club is more than a club. It's a repository for decades of history, for the hopes and fears and dreams of its players and supporters, for frustration and joy in equal measures (or unequal ones, depending on who you support). Every club is a community in itself. And of course every club has its own characteristics, which its fans defend to the hilt.

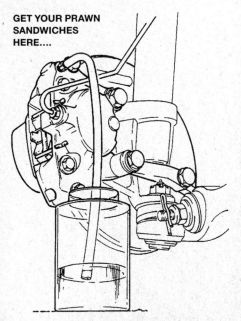

GET YOUR PRAWN SANDWICHES HERE....

FIG 12•8 **.... AND YOUR GLASS OF CHABLIS HERE. DON'T TELL ROY**

There's not nearly enough space in *Haynes Explains Football* to look at every club in the Premiership, let alone each one in all four divisions of the league. As an arbitrary cut-off point, here are the only six clubs never to have been relegated from the Premiership since it began in 1992 (which means there's no space for Manchester City, Leicester City and Blackburn Rovers, all of whom have been champions in that time).

1. Arsenal
Possessor of the longest-serving manager in football: Arsene Wenger has been there since approximately 1878. Subject of one of the best sports books ever written (*Fever Pitch*) and one of the most banal lyrics in pop history ('Arsenal team in the red and white/Mr Kevin Campbell and Ian Wright'). Nickname: the Gunners.

2. Chelsea
Notorious in the 1970s and 1980s for a hooligan problem so bad that even the club chairman suggested installing electric fences in the stadium. Since being bought by Russian gazillionaire Roman Abramovich, Chelsea have lived up much more to the affluent connotations of their name. Arguably more effective than pretty to watch.

3. Everton

To the outside world, perhaps most famous for being the Liverpool club which isn't Liverpool. The club where Wayne Rooney began his Premiership career and where he will almost certainly finish it too (while wearing Everton pyjamas throughout his time at Manchester United. Not on the pitch, obviously). Best nickname in the Premiership: the Toffees.

4. Liverpool

The dominant force of English (and European) football between the mid-70s and mid-80s, Liverpool have never quite hit those heights again (except on a May night in 2005 when they pulled off the Miracle of Istanbul). Reserves special affection for local boys made good such as Steven Gerrard and Jamie Carragher. Being at Anfield when they sing 'You'll Never Walk Alone' is an experience you'll never forget.

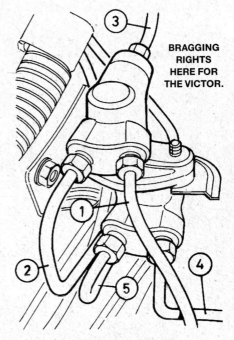

BRAGGING RIGHTS HERE FOR THE VICTOR.

FIG 12•9 **THE NORTH LONDON CONNECTION. PUTTING ARSENAL AND TOTTENHAM TOGETHER**

5. Manchester United

The team that everyone loves to hate (except those living in Surrey or Singapore, who are the club's biggest fans). The dominant force of the last 25 years, mostly under a manager so iconic he even had a timezone named after him. The only team ever to win the Treble. Prawn sandwiches often on the menu at Old Trafford, much to Roy Keane's disgust.

6. Tottenham Hotspur

Second in the Premiership for the last two seasons, though they've never won it. Often laboured in the shadow of North London rivals Arsenal. To cross from one to the other is seen by Spurs fans as the height of treachery: just ask Sol Campbell. Former club of Gary Lineker, Gazza and Garth Crooks, the only man in the world to ask longer questions than Noam Chomsky.

Vehicle league tables

1. Champions League

Used to be the European Cup and was only open to national champions. Now the Champions League with at least four places available to major nations and the chance to play clubs from places you've never heard of whose names would single-handedly win you Christmas Scrabble family games if you were allowed proper nouns. The TV coverage contains the insidious Handel-inspired earworm of 'the Champiooooons' after every ad break, and you are a stronger man than me if you don't find yourself inadvertently singing that at odd times.

2. Premiership

Usually the preserve of one or other of a handful of clubs – between them, Manchester United, Chelsea and Arsenal have won 21 of the Premiership's 25 titles – but now and then a surprise contender makes it through, and none have ever been or will probably ever be more surprising than Leicester City. Fun fact, trivia fans: if on 16 July 2015, when Donald Trump announced his candidacy for President, you'd put £10 on an accumulator of him winning, Jeremy Corbyn becoming Labour leader and Leicester winning the Premiership, you'd now be worth £66m.

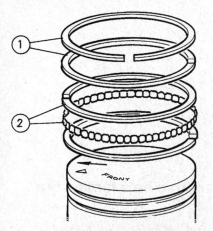

FIG 12•10 **PRELIMINARY ROUNDS AND GROUP STAGES: QUALIFYING CRITERIA FOR THE CHAMPIONS LEAGUE**

WARNING

If you support a club which has a realistic prospect of (a) winning the Premiership (b) finishing in the top four (c) being relegated, then nine months of your year will be consumed with working out endless permutations of what may happen in the league. By May, the words 'mathematically impossible' may spell either triumph ('to be relegated') or disaster ('to finish in the top four').

3. FA Cup

Before the rejigging of football in 1992 with the Champions League and Premiership taking over from the European Cup and First Division respectively, the FA Cup used to be huge. It wasn't just the prospect of lower-league clubs taking down bigger and better teams in giant-killings which would linger long in the memory, but also Cup Final day – the managers leading out their teams, the singing of 'Abide With Me', Wembley full of fans for whom this might be their team's one day in the sun after a glorious cup run. In recent years, much of this has gone. Though on the plus side there's still little to beat the sight of a lugubrious functionary, a superannuated player and a D-list celeb doing the draw for the next round of the Cup.

4. League Cup

This cup seems to change sponsors more often than most people change their underpants, but whoever's name is on the trophy, it's still a pretty rubbish competition, let's be honest. The big clubs still win it more often than not, mainly because they have better squads than everyone else and give their reserve team players a run-out (at least till the latter stages). And winning the League Cup means you get entry into next season's Europa League, which is basically a European-wide second-string cup itself.

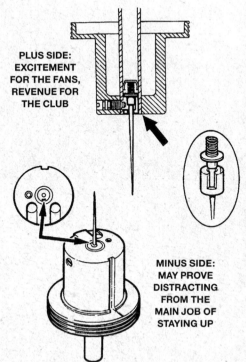

PLUS SIDE: EXCITEMENT FOR THE FANS, REVENUE FOR THE CLUB

MINUS SIDE: MAY PROVE DISTRACTING FROM THE MAIN JOB OF STAYING UP

FIG. 12•11 **WORKING OUT THE VALUE OF A DECENT CUP RUN**

The League Cup is like the annoying uncle you have to invite to the wedding because he's family, but even so no one really wants him there and no one really remembers him once he's left again.

Cooling system (fans)

Shakespeare spoke of the seven ages of man. Had football been around in his day (hang on, quick Wikipedia check, turns out it was in some form or another, though clearly *Match of the Day* wasn't around on account of neither Alan Hansen nor TV yet being invented), he would have amended that to the seven ages of being a football fan.

Going as a young kid with your Dad. Learning a lot of new words. Accepting the North Korean-style propaganda that Spurs/Arsenal, Liverpool/Everton or United/City (delete as appropriate) are the mortal enemy, just because.

Going as a teenager with your mates and without your Dad. Using those new words you learned which are no longer new. Being very sure not to use them in the direction of anyone who looks like they might be harder than you are (i.e. almost everyone).

For the die-hard fan, the year doesn't have four seasons. It has two. Football season, and the Waiting-for-football season

Going in your 20s. Beginning to talk sagely about the players of yesteryear, especially if you support a big club, in order to distinguish yourself from the Johnny-come-latelys who've watched a bit of Sky Sports and reckon that makes them lifelong fans.

Going in your 30s. The wheel of fortune will have turned at least once by now, so your team may either be enjoying unusual success or a worryingly barren spell. You like to think you accept these as inextricable parts of life. But you don't, not really.

Going in your 40s, now with an offspiring or two of your own. Having to explain to your children why the manager is a useless melonfarmer and the referee a total lockplucker.

Going in your 50s, and finding that your offspring now prefer to go with their own mates just as you did when you were their age, which is just as well as have you seen the price of tickets these days?

Going in your 60s and finding that you've been sitting alongside a bunch of blokes with stories very like your own for the best part of, well, 50 or 60 years.

⚠ The matchday experience

Arrive at ground. Hope you're not sitting next to the bloke who's really angry about everything and isn't afraid to let everyone know.

Good news: you're not sitting next to that bloke. Bad news: you're sitting right in front of him.

Receive some good-natured abuse from rival supporters. Realise it's not so good-natured. But it's definitely abuse.

Game kicks off. Your team proceeds to miss a number of chances that you're fairly sure your nan could have scored, and you don't mean that metaphorically.

A Plan day well in advance. Tickets. Transport. Mates.

You spend three hours in a tailback on the way home. Get home late, hungry and depressed. Vow never to do it again.

Opposition score with a minute to go. Angry Bloke explodes.

As the second half wears on, find yourself mildly awestruck by the relentlessness and creativity of Angry Bloke's rants.

Return to the stand. Find that Angry Bloke is even more angry than usual due to a missed penalty that you yourself missed.

B The opposition proves at least as useless as your own team, which is comforting in its own way. Half-time. Go to the toilets. Find that approximately 29,712 people have had the same idea as you. Make it to the urinal with a nanosecond to spare. Buy a pie. Spend 10 minutes trying to work out what kind of meat it is, and decide in the end that it's probably best if you don't know.

FIG 12•12

Audio system

Anthropologists will tell you that terrace chants are one of the last links to the oral traditions of folk music so prevalent in Britain before radio and TV. Whatevs. Either way, the breadth and depth of the terrace chant is quite something.

1) Some are funny (see page 23).
2) Some are offensive.
3) Some are both.
4) Some are taken from hymns, such as the 'glory glory [insert team name here]' from the *Battle Hymn Of The Republic*.

5) Some seem to come into being almost organically, such as the Italian fans adopting the White Stripes' 'Seven Nation Army' when their team won the 2006 World Cup.
6) And some are deeply moving: you don't have to be a Liverpool fan to find the hairs standing up on the back of your neck when you hear 50,000 people at Anfield singing 'You'll Never Walk Alone'.

One of the first things which fans of a winning team chant to fans of a losing team is 'you're not singing anymore.'

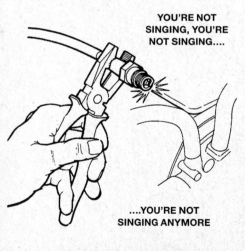

YOU'RE NOT SINGING, YOU'RE NOT SINGING....

....YOU'RE NOT SINGING ANYMORE

FIG 12•13 **CUT OFF IN THEIR PRIME: THE RELATIONSHIP BETWEEN SCOREBOARD AND AUDIENCE VOCALISATION.**

Blessing or curse

Being a fan is blessing and curse all in one go. There's the pride in your team, the joy of belonging to a tribe, and the let's-go-f***ing-mental moment when your side scores a winner in the 94th minute. Then there's the heartache at a bad result and the resigned knowledge that this season isn't going to be much cop either. As the man in the film said, it's not the despair. The despair you can live with. It's the hope which kills you.

⚠ Football chants

a) 'His name is Rio and he watches from the stand.' To the tune of 'Rio' by Duran Duran, and sung to Rio Ferdinand after he was banned for missing a drugs test.

b) 'When you're sat in row Z and the ball hits your head, that's Zamora, that's Zamora.' To the tune of 'That's Amore' by Dean Martin, and sung to West Ham/ Fulham/QPR striker Bobby Zamora on account of his wayward finishing.

c) 'He's fast, he's red, he talks like Father Ted, Robbie Keane, Robbie Keane.' Liverpool fans salute their Irish striker Robbie Keane.

d) 'Sunday, Monday, Habib Beye. Tuesday, Wednesday, Habib Beye. Thursday, Friday, Habib Beye. Saturday, Habib Beye, rocking all week with you!' To the tune of 'Happy Days', to Newcastle defender Habib Beye.

e) 'Podolski to the left of me, Walcott to the right, here I am, stuck in the middle Giroud.' To the tune of Stealers Wheel's 'Stuck In The Middle With You', by Arsenal fans to Olivier Giroud.

f) 'Juan Mata, two mata, three matarena.' To the tune of the Macarena, to Chelsea and Manchester United midfielder Juan Mata.

g) 'Neville Neville, they play in defence/ Neville Neville, their future's immense/ Neville Neville, they ain't half bad/ Neville Neville, the name of their Dad.' To the tune of David Bowie's 'Rebel Rebel', to Gary and Phil Neville at Manchester United (and their Dad really was called Neville Neville).

h) 'He's big, he's fast. his first name should come last, Stern John, Stern John.' To the tune of Quartermaster's Store, to Forest and Birmingham striker Stern John.

i) 'His name's a department store/ You know he's gonna score.' Bury fans to their striker Lenell John Lewis.

'You only live round the corner.' Fulham fans to Manchester United fans during a match.... at Fulham.

System control unit

Who'd be a football manager? Tons of stress, precious little job security (when the club chairman says you have his 'full confidence', you may as well start packing your bags), all the blame when you lose and little of the credit when you win, thousands of people thinking they can do your job better than you can, and to cap it all less pay than people think unless you're at a top club and/or have the England job. Managers come in all shapes and sizes. Here are a few:

1. The Enigmatic Foreigner

Especially if they don't speak much English, meaning their pronouncements are by definition gnomic and Yodaesque.

2. The Hipster Wunderkind

Younger than some of his players, or so it seems. Wears tight shirts, tighter trousers, cool glasses and switches between eight different languages in a press conference.

START: FULL OF HOPE AND NEW IDEAS. THE PLAYERS RISE TO THE OCCASION

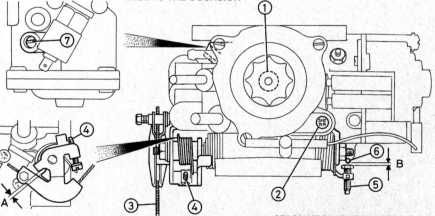

SUCCESS. YOU WIN SILVERWARE. THE FANS CHANT YOUR NAME

STAGNATION. THE SILVERWARE TARNISHES. THE FANS CHANT YOUR NAME, FOLLOWED BY THE WORD 'OUT'

FIG 12•14 **A MANAGER'S LIFESPAN: THE THREE STAGES OF RUNNING A CLUB**

3. The Former Great

A player for whom everything came easy. Management is the quickest way for them to find out that they might not be as good at dealing with people for whom everything doesn't come quite as easily.

4. The Club Legend

(May also be a Former Great.) Knows the place intimately. But again, this doesn't mean they'll be any good at being top dog. Would probably benefit from managing another club or two and getting some fresh ideas before returning home as the prodigal son.

5. The Bad Penny

Keeps on turning up. A year at this club, a couple of years at that club. Has never won anything of note, but somehow has fashioned a half-decent career. Perhaps it's because he gets the sack so often that he's almost always available for the next job. Or else he's got a lot of dirt on a lot of club chairmen.

6. The Caretaker

Long-serving deputy who gets his chance when the top man is sacked after picking up 3 points from a possible 30. Likely to prove more successful than his predecessor, which is a little embarrassing for all concerned.

7. The Sacrificial Lamb

The one who takes over from a long-serving legend. Never lasts long as always on a hiding to nothing. If he wins, it's because of systems already in place; if he loses, it's his own fault.

8. The Martinet

Considers himself as the headmaster and the players as unruly schoolboys, and therefore imposes endless draconian rules. Unlikely to end happily.

9. The Emotional One

The one who prowls the touchline, kicks every ball, makes every header, and provides highlights reels with plenty of material. It's a wonder when these guys make it past 45 without heart surgery.

One of the most enduring questions for the manager is this: tracksuit or business suit? Tracksuited managers like to look as though they could come on as a sub. Business-suited managers like to burnish their executive credentials. One thing's for sure: birthday suit is a no-no.

Global marketplace

The World Cup is (as the name suggests) the biggest prize in sport. It began in 1930 and has been played every four years since, barring the mild inconvenience of World War Two. Eight countries have won it: Brazil (5 times), Germany (4), Italy (4), Argentina (2), Uruguay (2), England (1), France (1) and Spain (1).

A: A GOLDEN GENERATION OF PLAYERS

B: A GOOD RIDE TO THE FINAL

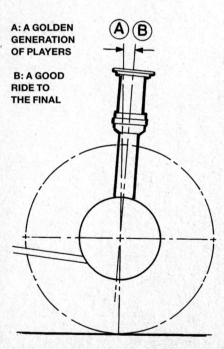

FIG 12•15 **PEAKING FOR THE WORLD CUP: A GUIDE TO NATIONAL GLORY**

1930

The first tournament. 13 teams compete. Uruguay win. Everyone involved thinks this World Cup malarkey might catch on.

1934

Italy host the event and prove not to be generous hosts in winning the thing. The four non-European teams (Brazil, Argentina, USA and Egypt) who make the long journey are all knocked out in the first round, and leave saying 'thanks a bunch' in four separate languages but one sarcastic tone.

1938

Italy win again. Mussolini is apparently very taken with seeing men in black shirts on the pitch before realising that they are the referees.

1950

Uruguay beat Brazil in the final in one of the greatest shocks in football history. Brazil retaliate by boycotting all Fray Bentos products.

1954

Germany beat Hungary in the 'Miracle of Bern'. It proves indeed miraculous, not least because it's the last time the Germans are either underdogs or popular winners.

1958
Brazil beat Sweden. A 17-year-old bloke scores two goals in the final and looks like he might be quite useful in a few years' time. His name is Pele.

1962
Chile and Italy play the 'battle of Santiago', which involves two players being sent off, mass brawls and police intervention – or, as travelling English fans think of it, a quiet Friday night in Portsmouth. Tensions are raised before the match when, in one of the most egregious pot/kettle/black examples in history, Italian journalists describe Santiago as a place where 'taxis are as rare as faithful husbands'.

1966
Italy manage to lose to North Korea. The players return home in the dead of night but are still pelted with rotten fruit by irate fans. In contrast, the North Koreans don't think the 1-0 victory is any big deal, since according to their state media they've already beaten Brazil 10-0, West Germany 12-1 and Argentina a thumping 32-3.

1970
Brazil skipper Carlos Alberto scores maybe the most joyful goal in World Cup history as his team beat Italy 4-1 in the final. You are not a real football fan if the skill and exuberance of that goal doesn't make you smile.

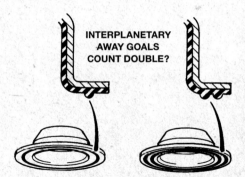

INTERPLANETARY AWAY GOALS COUNT DOUBLE?

FIG 12•16 **PICKING A WORLD XI TO PLAY MARS IN THE FLYING SAUCERS TOURNAMENT**

1974
The Netherlands, still smarting from Nazi occupation 30 years before, score in the first minute of the final against West Germany. The Germans win. But the Dutch are much cooler.

1978
Scottish manager Ally MacLeod says his team will definitely win the World Cup. In the group stage, they lose 3-1 to Peru and draw 1-1 with Iran. Scotland don't win the World Cup.

1982
West German goalkeeper Harald Schumacher breaks French defender Patrick Battiston's teeth and vertebrae with one of the worst challenges ever seen. In the final, Italian Marco Tardelli celebrates his goal by sprinting wildly yelling his own name, just as we all would in that position.

1986

Mexico hosts the tournament. The locals enliven tedious matches by standing up and sitting down in turn so that it looks like a wave is travelling round the stadium. Three decades on, scientists are still trying to come up with a name for this phenomenon.

1990

In the opening match, Cameroon defeat Argentina 1-0. Cameroonian defender Benjamin Massing is sent off for a tackle on Claudio Caniggia which is less a traditional foul than a judo throw. In the final, West Germany beat Argentina in one of the most boring matches ever played.

1994

The opening ceremony features Diana Ross taking a penalty. She manages to put the ball wide from about three metres out, thus earning her a call-up to the England squad.

1998

Dennis Bergkamp scores one of the great World Cup goals to beat Argentina in the quarter-finals. Dutch commentator Jack van Gelder, concerned that viewers might be unaware of the scorer's identity, screams 'Dennis Bergkamp! Dennis Bergkamp! Dennis Bergkamp! Dennis Bergkamp! Dennis Bergkamp! Dennis Bergkamp! Dennis Bergkamp!

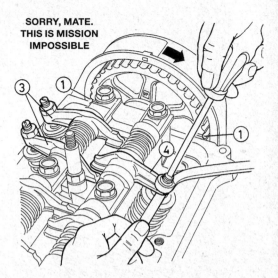

SORRY, MATE. THIS IS MISSION IMPOSSIBLE

FIG 12•17 **TRYING TO FIX THE ENGLAND TEAM'S PENALTY RADAR**

WARNING

World Cups can do strange things to your mind, health and viewing habits. 99 times out of 100, you wouldn't give Japan vs Algeria a second glance. You wouldn't even know they were playing. But because it's a World Cup you HAVE to watch it, you HAVE to know everything about the players involved, and you HAVE to pick a side to root for and be gutted when they lose in the 89th minute.

2002

Mild-mannered Roy Keane flies home after an argument with Ireland manager Mick McCarthy. Keane tells his manager 'I didn't rate you as a player, I don't rate you as a manager and I don't rate you as a person. You can stick your World Cup up your arse.' Say what you mean, Roy.

2006

Zinedine Zidane headbutts Marco Materazzi in the final and is sent off. Rather than admonish him for this, most of Zidane's countrymen applaud this display of pluperfect Frenchness. World Cups come and go. Decking someone who's insulted your sister is for ever.

2010

South African fans introduce the world to the vuvuzela, a plastic horn which produces a monotone so loud and annoying that scientists could have worked 50 years on producing just that sound without ever getting it so perfect.

No one knows who won the tournament in 2010 as every spectator had been driven to insanity by the sound of vuvuzelas long before the final.

2014

Feeling peckish during Uruguay's match against Italy, Luis Suárez bites Giorgio Chiellini. Suárez later claims that Chiellini 'bumped into me with his shoulder, leaving a small bruise on my cheek and a strong pain in my teeth'. As far as explanations go, this is right up there with Japanese emperor Hirohito's explanation after his country's unconditional surrender in 1945 that 'the war situation has developed, not necessarily to Japan's advantage.'

ENSURE ENDLESS SUPPLY OF IMPORTED LAGER HERE...

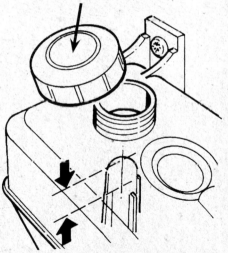

... AND ENDLESS SUPPLY OF FLAVOURED CRISPS HERE

FIG 12•18 **A WORLD CUP VIEWING KIT: THE FANS' ESSENTIALS**

The lingo

Football has a language all of its own. Goals, for example, can't just be scored: they must be belted, blasted, curled, drilled, fired, hammered, lashed, leathered, rifled, slotted, smashed or thundered. Headers can be glanced, steered or thumped. Deflections are always wicked, volleys acrobatic, penalties converted, finishes clinical, chips impudent, lobs audacious, backheels cheeky and passes slide rule. Football even has its own tenses, whether it's 'he's gone and given it away' or 'the lads done well'.

Here, *Haynes Explains Football* provides a list of common football clichés. It's not exhaustive, but it should see you through 95% of football-related conversations. Deploy these with confidence and no one will know whether or not you're bluffing.

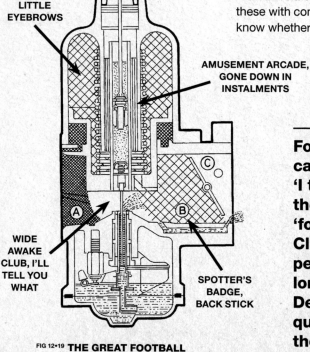

EARLY DOORS, LITTLE EYEBROWS

AMUSEMENT ARCADE, GONE DOWN IN INSTALMENTS

WIDE AWAKE CLUB, I'LL TELL YOU WHAT

SPOTTER'S BADGE, BACK STICK

FIG 12•19 **THE GREAT FOOTBALL LEXICOGRAPHICAL GENERATOR**

Football pundits can never say 'I think': instead, they always say 'for me'. 'For me, Clive, that's a penalty all day long.' 'For me, Des, they're not quick enough at the back.' 'For me, therefore I am.'

⚠ A guide to football clichés

Clichés	Description
110%	Standard measurement of effort.
Best fans in the world	We don't win very often.
Big	What a goalkeeper must make himself when in a one-on-one.
Dressing room, lose the	Of a manager, to no longer command the respect of his players. Not a literal statement.
End of the day	Point in time for all footballers. Can occur at any time of day.
Gets into great positions	Couldn't hit a cow's arse with a banjo.
Given, seen them	The referee was erroneous in not awarding a penalty.
Great engine	Runs around like a headless chicken.
[insert town name], wet February night in	The time, place and climatic conditions when you find out whether fancy-dan foreigners can hack it in English football.
Handbags	A confrontation between opposing players.
'I didn't see the incident'	It was a stonewall penalty against my team.
Mercurial	Temperamental and lazy.
Natural goalscorer	Greedy bastard.
Reads the game well	Slow.
Row Z	Far-flung location in the stands which is the ultimate destination of a forceful defensive clearance.
Run it off	Traditional method of treating any injury.
Strong in the air	Has two left feet.
Super Sunday	Sunday.
Too good to go down	Belief that a team's ability will preclude it from relegation.
Two halves, a game of	We were well on top and got too complacent.
Union	Unofficial organisation of goalkeepers.
Unsung hero	Everyone except the manager thinks he's crap.

Domestic industry

1872
England play their first international match, a friendly against Scotland. Sorry: a 'friendly' against Scotland. The team includes players from Oxford University and the 1st Surrey Rifles.

1908
England play their first European opposition, beating Austria, Hungary and Bohemia. The latter result inspires a famous Queen song. Maybe.

1950
England play in the World Cup for the first time and manage to lose 1-0 to the USA.

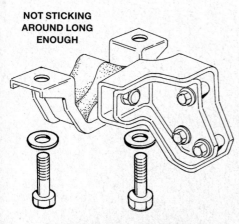

NOT STICKING AROUND LONG ENOUGH

FIG 12•20 **SCREWING IT UP – EVERY ENGLAND WORLD CUP CAMPAIGN BAR 1966**

1953
Hungary beat England 6-3 in London and 7-1 in Budapest. England centre-half Syd Owen said 'It was like playing people from outer space.' Hopefully he said it in the kind of bewildered tone later adopted by his near namesake Sid Owen, who played Ricky in *Eastenders*.

1966
England win the World Cup on home soil, a feat which in no way looms large over every subsequent England team. Subtract 1966 from whatever the current year is: that's how many years of hurt. A monstrously hungover Jack Charlton wakes up the next morning on a stranger's sofa in Leytonstone. Different times.

1982
Bryan Robson scores the quickest goal in World Cup history against France. England are eliminated without losing a game. A very English way to go out.

1986
England lose to Diego Maradona in the World Cup quarter-final. One 'Hand of God' goal, one mesmerising slalom from the halfway line. 'You have to say that's magnificent,' said Barry Davies about the second goal. Not all English supporters were so charitable.

1990

England go out on penalties to West Germany. Chris Waddle's final kick is spotted by *Voyager 1* somewhere around Saturn shortly before going interstellar.

1992

England lose to the Swedes. *The Sun* calls manager Graham Taylor a 'turnip'. Basically the best edition of *Gardener's World* ever.

1996

Football comes home during Euro 96. Again England meet the Germans in the semi-finals. Again there's a penalty shootout. Can you guess what happened next?

1998

Michael Owen scores a wonder goal against Argentina. David Beckham is sent off. The match goes to extra time. And then penalties. And… this is just too depressing to keep writing about.

2001

England beat Germany 5-1 in Munich. No-one can quite believe it. Least of all the Germans. Even Emile Heskey scores.

2004

England go out of Euro 2004 on penalties to Portugal.

2006

England go out of the World Cup on penalties to Portugal.

2008

Good news: England don't go out of Euro 2008 on penalties to Portugal. Bad news: only because they didn't qualify for Euro 2008 in the first place.

2010

England go out of the World Cup to Germany. But not on penalties, just to mix things up a bit. A comprehensive 4-1 thumping.

2012

Normal service resumed at Euro 2012. Another penalty shootout, this time against Italy. England win. Only joking.

2014

England fail to progress from their World Cup group. While in Brazil, they make an emotional visit to an orphanage. 'Look at their sad little faces, devoid of hope,' said Jose, aged 6.

2016

England are eliminated from Euro 2016 by Iceland. Yes, Iceland. Fancying their chances, several other supermarket chains challenge England to a match. A couple of petrol station mini-marts and the newsagents on the corner of York Road and Garfield Avenue fancy their chances too.

⚠ Fault diagnosis

Fault	Diagnosis	Treatment
One of your players is a lunatic	He's the goalkeeper	They're all like that. Sorry.
You can't play Total Football	You're neither Dutch nor very good	Go back to 4-4-2, there's a good boy.
Referee has made the wrong decision	Referee needs glasses	Referee should go to Specsavers.
Opposition player is wearing lurid yellow boots	Opposition player is a flash git	Give him a good kicking.
It feels like you're running through treacle	It's Sunday morning and you have a hangover	Keep sweating it out. You'll be fine after half-time.
Everyone hates the team you support	You support Manchester United	They'll hate you anyway, so you might as well try and beat them.
You're in a crowd of people who seem to have Tourette's	You're on the terraces at a football match and the game is not going your team's way	Either leave or accept it'll all be over soon enough anyway.
You need the toilet urgently	You have drunk several pints before the game started	Head towards exit 28 now.
Sixty million people think they can do your job better than you can	You are the England manager	Proceed to next major tournament. Suffer humiliating defeat by Andorra, Montserrat or Vanuatu.
You have total control of players who are doing impossibly brilliant things.	You are playing FIFA on Playstation	Turn off the TV and return to normal life.
You've lost a yard of pace	You never had that yard of pace in the first place	Ponder whether this is satisfactory or unsatisfactory.
England have gone out of a football tournament	England have been forced to undergo a penalty shootout	No treatment available. Just accept it as part of the yawning futility of existence.

Conclusion

Former Liverpool manager Bill Shankly famously said that 'football is not a matter of life and death. It's more important than that.' It has helped start wars (El Salvador and Honduras in 1969) and provided humanity during them (the Christmas Day match between German and British soldiers in World War One.) Harold Wilson said that the shock and loss of national prestige caused by England's defeat to West Germany in the 1970 World Cup helped him lose the general election three days later. It has been used for naked political purposes (Argentina's ruling junta doing their best to ensure that the national team won their home World Cup in 1978).

Football can bring together and it can divide. After an England victory, particularly against an old enemy such as Argentina or Germany, the national mood visibly lifts. You can smile at a stranger in the street without them thinking you're insane, trying to come onto them or distracting them while someone else picks their pocket. It's strange how the fortunes of 11 people you've almost certainly never met and with whom you share little bar a passport can so affect your life, but there it is.

Humans are tribal people and football is a tribal game. We define ourselves not just by who we support but also by who we oppose. It's not for nothing that the greatest victories are the ones against the greatest rivals, be it in terms of success (two teams going for the title) or geography – there's always some spice to a local derby. Which begs the question: when Derby County play Nottingham Forest, is it a Derby derby? And what happens if Josie d'Arby attends the match wearing a derby hat?

Most of us have played it at one time or another, no matter how well or badly (or how great the difference between how good we think we are and how good we actually are). It's a pig's bladder and an onion bag at the end of the day, Des. Funny old game of two halves.

Few people live their lives totally untouched by football. It's on TV, it's the topic of conversations round the watercooler and in the pub, it's impromptu games in the park on a summer evening and five-a-side leagues up and down the country.

Titles in the Haynes Explains series

Now that Haynes has explained Football, you can progress to our full size manuals on car maintenance (DIY Rovers), *Men's Pie Manual* (who ate them all?), *Dance Manual* (everything but dabbing) and *Modern Man Manual* (style it like Beckham).

There are Haynes manuals on just about everything – but let us know if we've missed one.

Haynes.com